Grayslake Area Public Library District
Grayslake, Illinois

LeBron James

by Josh Gregory

Consultant: Charlie Zegers
Sports Journalist

New York, New York

Credits

Cover and Title Page, © Wilfredo Lee/AP Images, © Ed Suba Jr./AP Images, and © Robbins Photography; 4, © Lynne Sladky/AP Images; 5, © Mike Segar/AP Images; 6, © Amy Sancetta/AP Images; 7, © Amy Sancetta/AP Images; 8, © Kirthmon Dozier/AP Images; 9, © Mark Duncan/AP Images; 10, © Ed Betz/AP Images; 11, © Candace Beckwith/Dreamstime.com; 12, © Robbins Photography; 13, © Robbins Photography; 14, © Lynne Sladky/AP Images; 15, © Domenic Gareri/Shutterstock, Inc.; 16, © Alex Menendez/AP Images; 17, © Ed Suba Jr./AP Images; 18, © Helga Esteb/Shutterstock, Inc.; 19, © Bruce Schwartzman/AP Images; 20, © Phil Long/AP Images; 21, © Eric Gay/AP Images; 22, © Robbins Photography.

Publisher: Kenn Goin
Editor: Jessica Rudolph
Creative Director: Spencer Brinker
Photo Researcher: Josh Gregory

Library of Congress Cataloging-in-Publication Data

Gregory, Josh.
  Lebron James / by Josh Gregory.
    pages cm. — (Basketball heroes making a difference)
  Includes bibliographical references and index.
  ISBN 978-1-62724-082-6 (library binding) — ISBN 1-62724-082-9 (library binding)
  1. James, LeBron—Juvenile literature. 2. Basketball players—United States—Biography—Juvenile literature. 3. African American basketball players—Biography—Juvenile literature. I. Title.
  GV884.J36G74 2014
  796.323092—dc23
  [B]
                                    2013037786

For more information, write to Bearport Publishing Company, Inc., 45 West 21st Street, Suite 3B, New York, New York 10010. Printed in the United States of America.

10 9 8 7 6 5 4 3 2 1

Contents

Just Seconds Left

It was the final showdown of the 2012–2013 season: **Game 7** of the **NBA** Finals. The Miami Heat faced the San Antonio Spurs. With just under 30 seconds left in the game, the Heat were ahead by only two points. The score was so close that either team could still win the 2013 NBA championship.

The Heat's biggest star, LeBron James, sank a 19-foot (5.8 m) jump shot. The score was now 92–88. On the next play, after LeBron stole the ball, a Spurs player immediately **fouled** him. Now he had a chance to shoot two **free throws**. The crowd roared, but LeBron kept his cool. Both shots went in. The score was now 94–88. The Spurs had no time for a **comeback**. The Heat had won their second championship in a row!

LeBron (right) playing in Game 7 of the 2013 NBA Finals

LeBron (center) scored 37 points to defeat the Spurs, tying the all-time record for points scored in Game 7 of the NBA Finals.

LeBron was named the most valuable player (MVP) of both the 2012 and 2013 NBA Finals.

A Shooting Star

Long before he was an NBA superstar, LeBron shot hoops on basketball courts in Akron, Ohio. Life was not always easy for young LeBron. His father was not around to help raise him. Sometimes, his mother, Gloria, could not find work. The family often lived in neighborhoods where crime was a problem. "It was a struggle," LeBron later said, "but at the end of the day, it made me become who I am today."

LeBron stayed out of trouble by getting involved with basketball. He rode his bike to different courts in Akron and practiced whenever he could. By the time he was in eighth grade, his scoring and **rebounding** skills had made him well known throughout the city.

LeBron poses with his mother, Gloria, after receiving the NBA's MVP award in 2009.

When LeBron was 12 years old, he and four of his friends formed a basketball team called the Shooting Stars.

LeBron (left) is still friends with Dru Joyce III (center) and Siam Cotton (right), two of his teammates on the Shooting Stars.

Whiz Kid

As a teenager, LeBron's height, strength, and speed helped him rise as a basketball star at Saint Vincent–Saint Mary High School. When he was just a freshman, LeBron made the school's **varsity** basketball team. He led the team, the Fighting Irish, to an undefeated season and a state championship.

By his sophomore year, LeBron had so many fans that Saint Vincent–Saint Mary had to play some of its games at a nearby college with more seating. Around 5,000 fans crowded into the college's arena. Over the next three years, LeBron grew more famous. Some of his high school games were broadcast on national television. NBA stars such as Shaquille O'Neal even stopped by the arena to watch him play!

LeBron chose to wear the number 23 on his jersey in honor of his hero, basketball legend Michael Jordan (shown here), who also wore the number 23.

During his four years at Saint Vincent–Saint Mary, LeBron scored 2,657 points and grabbed 892 rebounds.

At the age of 16, LeBron already stood six feet seven inches (2 m) tall.

Going Pro

Many NBA teams wanted LeBron to play for them as soon as he graduated high school. As a result, he chose to enter the 2003 NBA **draft** instead of attending college. That year, the Cleveland Cavaliers, also known as the Cavs, had the first pick. They chose LeBron over every other player who entered the draft.

LeBron was thrilled that the Cavs picked him. Playing for a team in Ohio meant that he could stay near his friends and family. However, LeBron was also under a lot of pressure. Many basketball fans believed that he would be the NBA's next big star. They even compared him to his hero, Michael Jordan. Would he be able to live up to their expectations?

LeBron shaking hands with NBA Commissioner David Stern after being picked first in the 2003 draft

LeBron has played the position of **forward** throughout his NBA career.

A Star from the Start

It didn't take long for LeBron to show off his skills. During his **rookie season**, he led his Cavs teammates in points scored per game. LeBron even set a record as the youngest NBA player to score more than 40 points in a single game.

LeBron was more than just a great scorer, however. His height, long arms, and quick thinking made him a leader in rebounds. His skillful passing also made him a great team player. A year before LeBron joined the Cavs, they had finished in fifteenth place in the **Eastern Conference**. The following season, LeBron helped them reach ninth place. In just one season, he had become one of the NBA's brightest stars.

LeBron warms up before a game against the Milwaukee Bucks during his rookie season.

The Cavaliers improved from a 17–65 record in the 2002–2003 season to a 35–47 record in LeBron's rookie season.

LeBron was named the NBA's 2003–2004 Rookie of the Year. He was the first Cavs player ever to win this award.

A Move to Miami

With LeBron leading the team, the Cavs improved over the next several years. In the 2008–2009 and 2009–2010 seasons, they had the best record in the Eastern Conference. LeBron was named the NBA's MVP both seasons. However, the Cavs lost in the **playoffs** both times, failing to reach the NBA Finals.

By this time, many people already considered LeBron to be one of the best basketball players of all time. However, he had never won an NBA championship. LeBron had a tough decision. Would he have a better chance of achieving his goal if he left the Cavs for a different team? In 2010, LeBron joined the Miami Heat. In Florida, he would get to play alongside fellow superstars Chris Bosh and Dwyane Wade.

LeBron chose to play for the Miami Heat because he knew that he would need skilled teammates like Dwyane Wade (left) to help him win an NBA championship.

LeBron changed his jersey number from 23 to 6 when he joined the Heat.

LeBron announced his decision to join the Miami Heat on live television on July 8, 2010. Millions of basketball fans across the country watched the broadcast.

Hometown Hero

Though LeBron no longer plays in Ohio, he has not forgotten his home. Today, he helps run the LeBron James Family Foundation (LJFF). Through the LJFF, LeBron supports **charities** such as Wheels for Education and the Boys and Girls Clubs of America.

LeBron works with Wheels for Education to make sure that Akron's students stay in school. Each year, LeBron meets with a group of third graders in Akron to discuss the importance of education. If the students work hard and get good grades, they are rewarded with laptop computers, school supplies, and bicycles. Being able to offer students bicycles means a lot to LeBron. "I'll never forget the day I got my first bike," he says. "It was like being handed keys to the world."

LeBron with kids from the Boys and Girls Clubs of America

The Boys and Girls Clubs of America offer after-school programs such as sports and art classes.

LeBron speaks to a group of students in his Wheels for Education program.

Back to School

Because LeBron's hometown roots are so important to him, he also works to support the students at Saint Vincent–Saint Mary High School. In 2013, LeBron returned to his old school. At a special assembly, he promised to provide brand-new uniforms for each of the school's sports teams.

LeBron still remembers when Saint Vincent–Saint Mary's arena couldn't hold all the fans who wanted to see him play. As a result, he is also helping to **renovate** the high school's basketball arena. He has given $1 million to build new bleachers, locker rooms, flooring, and more.

LeBron's wife, Savannah, plays an active role in the LJFF. For instance, in 2013, she donated prom dresses to around 100 underprivileged girls in Akron and Miami.

LeBron, shown here playing basketball in high school, helped oversee the planning of the new arena at Saint Vincent–Saint Mary.

When it opens, the new arena at Saint Vincent–Saint Mary will be known as the LeBron James Arena.

A Living Legend

LeBron James is one of the most legendary players in the NBA. Since joining the Heat, he has helped the team win two NBA championships. However, giving back to his hometown of Akron, Ohio, is just as important to him. "I was born here, I was raised here, and no matter where my work takes me, my family and I will always call this great city our home," says LeBron.

Whether he is making headlines for his remarkable performance on the court or for taking the time to help kids in Akron, LeBron is a true basketball hero. With many more seasons ahead of him, there's no telling what he will accomplish.

LeBron's Wheels for Education program grew out of a cycling event he started, in which people in Akron rode 2.6 miles (4.2 km) to raise money for charity. Here, LeBron rides alongside participants in the 2010 event.

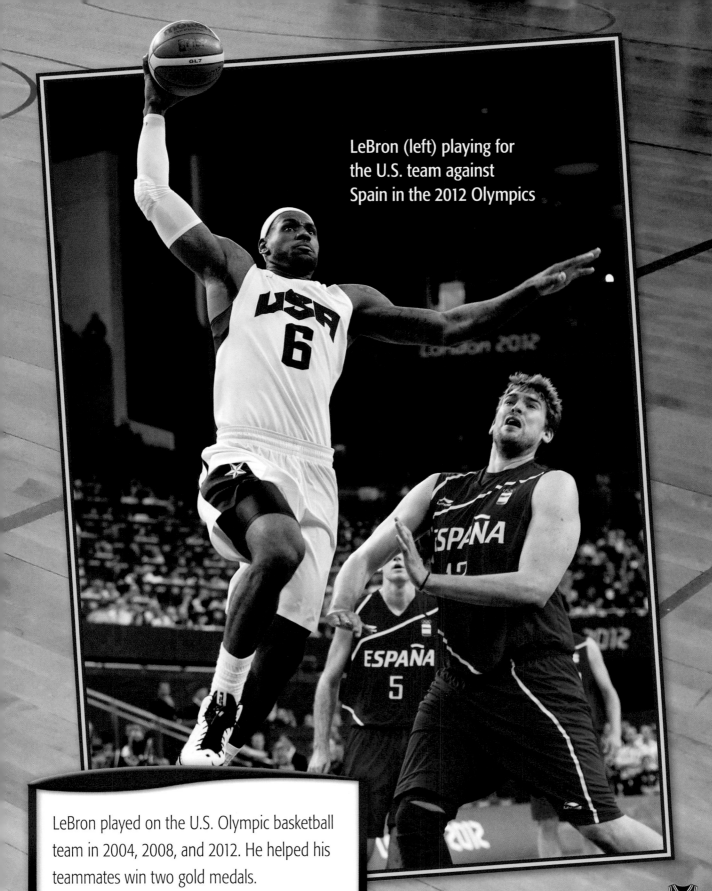

LeBron (left) playing for the U.S. team against Spain in the 2012 Olympics

LeBron played on the U.S. Olympic basketball team in 2004, 2008, and 2012. He helped his teammates win two gold medals.

The LeBron File

LeBron is a basketball hero on and off the court. Here are some highlights.

MIAMI HEAT

- In a 2013 game against the Portland Trail Blazers, LeBron set an NBA record by scoring 30 points and making at least 60 percent of his shots in six straight regular season games.

- LeBron's fans often call him by the nickname *King James*.

- LeBron is able to shoot and handle a basketball almost equally as well with either his right or left hand. LeBron developed this ability by practicing his shots with both hands when he was very young.

Glossary

charities (CHA-ruh-teez) groups that try to help people in need

comeback (KUHM-bak) a situation in which a team that is losing quickly scores enough points to close the gap

draft (DRAFT) an event in which professional teams take turns choosing new athletes to play for them

Eastern Conference (EES-turn KAHN-fur-uhnss) one of two 15-team divisions making up the NBA

forward (FOR-wurd) one of the standard positions on a basketball team that is often responsible for much of the team's scoring; a team's two forwards are generally taller than the guards but shorter than the team's center

fouled (FOWLD) hit or interfered with in a manner that is against the rules

free throws (FREE THROHZ) attempts to make a basket given to a player who has been fouled

Game 7 (GAYM SEHV-uhn) the final game of a seven-game NBA playoff series; two teams enter the game with three wins each, and the winner of the game will win the series

NBA (EHN-BEE-AY) letters standing for the National Basketball Association, the professional men's basketball league in North America

playoffs (PLAY-awfss) a series of games that determine which teams will play in a championship

rebounding (REE-bound-ing) catching a basketball after a missed shot

renovate (REN-uh-vayt) to improve the condition of something

rookie season (RUK-ee SEE-zuhn) the first year that a person plays as a professional athlete

varsity (VAR-suh-tee) the athletes at a university or other school who are the best at their sport

Bibliography

Hochman, Benjamin. "LeBron James' Choice Puts Miami Back in the Game." *Denver Post* (July 9, 2010).

Simmons, Bill. "LeBron Makes LeLeap." Grantland.com (June 22, 2012).

Theiss, Evelyn. "LeBron James in Akron to Honor Kids in His 'Wheels for Education' Program." *The Plain Dealer* (August 19, 2012).

Read More

Christopher, Matt. *On the Court with . . . LeBron James.* New York: Little Brown (2008).

Sandler, Michael. *LeBron James: I Love Challenges! (Defining Moments: Super Athletes).* New York: Bearport (2009).

Savage, Jeff. *LeBron James (Amazing Athletes).* Minneapolis, MN: Lerner (2014).

Learn More Online

To learn more about LeBron James and the Miami Heat, visit
www.bearportpublishing.com/BasketballHeroes

Index

24